THE
SEASONAL HOME

THE
SEASONAL HOME

Decorating ideas inspired by the seasons

Kristin Perers

Photography by James Merrell

RYLAND
PETERS
& SMALL

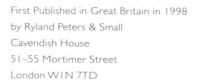

To my Mom and Dad, who gave me a childhood home so grounded in love that it gave me the freedom to fly

Designers **Mark Latter and Vicky Holmes**
Senior Editor **Sian Parkhouse**
Stylist **Kristin Perers**
Illustrator **Kristin Perers**
Creative Director **Jacqui Small**
Publishing Director **Anne Ryland**

First Published in Great Britain in 1998
by Ryland Peters & Small
Cavendish House
51–55 Mortimer Street
London W1N 7TD

The publishers are grateful for permission to quote
extracts from the following books:
p.8 *The Prophet* by Kahlil Gibran, Borzoi Books/Alfred A.
Knopf, copyright © Kahlil Gibran 1923, 1951 (renewal by
Administrators C.T.A. of Kahlil Gibran Estate, and Mary G.
Gibran); pp. 12 and 14 *Shelter for the Spirit* by Victoria
Moran, HarperCollins*Publishers* copyright © 1997 Victoria
Moran

Printed and bound in China by Toppan Printing Co.

ISBN 1 900518 68 6

A CIP record for this book is available from the British
Library

Contents

Inspirations

'Your house shall not be an anchor but a mast'

Kahlil Gibran

Each season brings a different mood. The temperature and the quality of the light change: we want to feel cool and easy in summer and warm and cosy in winter. The seasons have an inevitable rhythm, but this can be lost in our modern lives, especially in the city. We now have electricity that allows us to work all night. Heating and air conditioning serve as instant temperature controls. These modern conveniences have certainly added to our lives but we are in danger of losing something as well – if we are not careful we could lose the harmony and balance that nature provides. Nature has its own pace, it can't be rushed: part of its beauty is in the process of time unfolding. What are the seasons but a play of opposites? The freedom of summer is a reaction to the hibernation of winter. Both heat and cold have their place, and darkness and shadow makes us appreciate lengthening days all the more. The

Everyday wonders

anticipation of the first strawberries is what heightens their sweetness. Let your home have visual prompts for the feelings that each season brings. Why is it is in spring that we feel the need to throw open our windows and do a clean sweep of the house? It is a reaction to the months of being shut inside. In summer we relax and mentally if not physically we go on holiday. In the autumn we tidy up the year and try to complete all the tasks that have not been finished and winter is time to look inward at our thoughts. Change is the only constant: apply this to your life and your home and use it as a reminder to observe the everyday wonders around you. Our responses to our external environment are what make a house a living home. Sometimes those responses can be small personal gestures, sometimes they are bold single strokes that make a room come alive. Details that evoke the seasons change the spirit of a room, allowing you and your home to be connected to the natural rhythm of the earth.

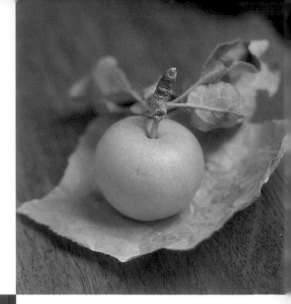

create seasonal still lifes

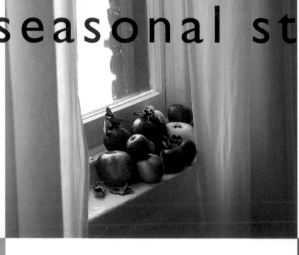

It is on walks that a lot of my own inspiration comes. Be it through a city park, a woodland glade or along the seashore, I take in the sights and sounds, smells and textures of each changing season, collecting charms as I go to take home as a reminder of the natural world. These collections become a

revolving display in my home, to be savoured and enjoyed for a while and then changed and replenished as the seasons do. Your home is a blank canvas. It's fun to create tabletop still lifes by combining your favourite finds: twigs from last weekend's country walk, a simple jug filled with sweet peas fresh from the garden. Extend your enjoyment of your outdoor experience.

five environmental factors that influence our well being:

light

sound

aroma

colour

touch

I'm a true believer in the power of beauty. It can inspire, heal and awaken your senses. Others may trivialize the importance of a pretty flower display but I know what it does to my heart. Beauty is the gift the world gives us. A scent can immediately bring back long-forgotten memories. Sunlight on your skin after a long winter can chase away any cares. Your surroundings hold tremendous power on your moods and emotions so use that power for positive effect.

nature gives us the variety we crave

'Discover sacred space in the midst of the ordinary and realize that the ordinary has been extraordinary all along.'

Victoria Moran, Shelter for the Spirit

'Summer is disruptive – too much heat and too much activity. But in the fall there is order, in winter there is tradition, and in the spring there is growth. Spring is when I'm needed by my rose bushes and the grass and the flowers. I renew my house and it renews me.'

Toni, Shelter for the Spirit

let what's going on outside influence what's going on inside

The garden and the vegetable market are great sources of inspiration. Follow the colours that nature offers each season. Watch how changing a vase of flowers from summer daisies to autumnal hydrangeas can alter the mood of a room. This simple change will leave you wanting to put away the breezy linens of summer and throw a rich

bring the whole beach
home in just one pebble

paisley shawl over the sofa, and then move the furniture closer to the fire. One change leads to another. Think of the joy of bringing home an armful of sunflowers and the first strawberries of the season. Place these on your kitchen table and there is no doubt summer has arrived!

'The best
things
in life
are free.'

Spring plays hide and seek with us – here one day and gone the next. We can't quite put away our winter woollens but we are yearning for a change, a freshness, to mark the birth of the new year that is upon us. No other season is waited for with such hope and anticipation. The first warm days send us outside smiling again. The earth sends up a rush of growth and the world is young again. What are the essential elements that evoke this season? Imagine the surprise of colour from the first crocus blooms, the heavenly scent of lily of the valley or the

spring

song of birds returning to the garden. The world is full of potential. It's a delicate time, a time of renewal, when nature gives birth. Find creative ways to bring this excitement indoors. Forcing bulbs is one of the easiest and most satisfying of spring time pleasures. Use your imagination when looking for containers – you'll find a whole host of ideas in ordinary things you already have around the house. An old metal bucket can be loaded with Paperwhites, inexpensive enamel mugs look charming in a row with a hyacinth blooming in each.

Small branches of fruit trees such as cherry, quince and apple can be brought indoors for forcing. Split the ends of the woody stems, stand them in water in a warm room and watch the blossom open. Seeds should be sorted and started for the earliest flowers and herbs. Sow them in traditional wooden seed trays on a light window sill. The emerging buds are a reminder of earth's renewal.

The textures of spring are warm and welcoming – think of the softness of pussy willow buds or the fluff of a newly hatched chick. Tender ferns curl up from the wet earth. Take a cue from this and surround yourself with soft cotton knits, beautifully worn and faded floral chintzes, innocent gingham checks: all these fabrics reflect the delicate world that is emerging outside. Introduce soft colours in your home that reflect nature's palette, such as shades of lilac, dusty pink and green. A splash of yellow daffodils on your kitchen table can in one stroke banish all memories of winter.

Traditionally, it is a time to do a clean sweep of the house, shake off the dust and freshen the home. Wash the windows to let the longer daylight shine in. Use natural cleaning materials such as white vinegar, baking soda and borax to ensure a healthy home as well as a clean one. Scrub wooden surfaces with beeswax polish for a glowing patina and a wonderful lingering scent.

The air is charged with energy and optimism. The change in the weather urges us to come out of hibernation and socialize again. Be inspired by the new season's produce coming onto the market. and plan a meal around the surprises of spring. The subtle flavour of new potatoes with fresh mint and the youngest peas will not be repeated again in the year. Indulge yourself with fleeting seasonal pleasures and toss salads with freshly picked violets. Catch a dose of spring fever and let your home burst forward with the same vibrancy as the season outside.

As the days lengthen the light gets stronger, the weather warmer and summer is here. The elements make us feel like relaxing, mentally winding down. Summer is about freedom. Freedom from routine, freedom even from the constraints of clothes. Life takes on a more laid-back approach. Summer decorating should reflect this and at its best be like going on holiday, easy and relaxing. Surrender to the season and simplify the home, giving yourself some breathing space. In summer the house becomes a shady retreat from the scorching

summer

weather outside. It's time to lighten the house, open windows, pare down bedding to a minimum. Roll rugs away and let bare feet run across cool floorboards. Change your curtains to sheer white linen. Improvise and use a straw beach mat as a table runner or make a centrepiece of a bowl filled with sea glass found on a walk. A single starfish looks enchanting on a window sill silhouetted against a brilliant blue sky. Fling a crocheted shawl over a table and place a vase on top overflowing with cow parsley. Summer is gone in a flash so grab it while you can.

Be freespirited with your home and let it be as spontaneous as the season. Move some furniture outside and create areas for enjoying the delights of the summer sunshine. A daybed on the porch piled with cushions and enveloped in mosquito netting, or a huge canvas hammock strung between two shady trees, are all you need to entice you into a lazy day's reading.

Summer starts delicately and grows bolder as the season progresses. Outside colours become more intense to stand up to the stronger sunlight. Take a cue from the fuchsia cosmos growing in your garden and add stronger accents indoors. Let it be as simple as a bowl of nectarines or a pot of marigolds. Flowers are in abundance at this time of year so don't hold back. Make full clusters of flowers arranged in a casual way as they would naturally grow in the garden. And herbs needn't be reserved for the kitchen and cooking. Mix mint, rosemary and sage in with your flower arrangements or grow them in a bedroom window box. The scent through an open window at night will assure plenty of sweet dreams.

Cooking becomes an outdoor activity inspired by southern climates. From croissants on the porch to clam bakes in the evening we want to spend every waking minute outside. Even if you are stuck in the city for the summer you can transport yourself temporarily by cooking a meal inspired by the destination of your choice. With the availability of ingredients and produce from all over the world today its easy to bring home the taste, scents and colours of almost any exotic land. Creating a romantic atmosphere for dining al fresco can be as easy as throwing a few cushions and a tablecloth outside, and filling jam jars with sand and lighting candles in them. All you need is a few shooting stars to finish off the night.

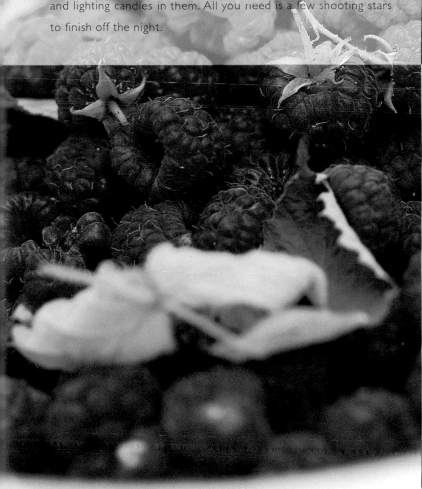

Beachcombing

To look closely at a handful of sea glass is to look at the sea. Sea glass has all the elements of the sea: the colour, the frosty texture and worn salt-like transparency all convey the combination of sea, sand and light. One piece alone shimmers like sunlight on water, and in combination the various colours bounce off each other like an entire seaside landscape. Gathering these little jewels on waterside walks is a natural enjoyment for children and adults alike. A handful brought home can serve as a reminder of the sea in much the same way that a painting or photograph would. I love strolling along creating mini colour palettes in my hand as I go. I'm always amazed at how nature sets out groups of colours that balance and play off each other perfectly. I add and edit as I walk, enjoying the way a palette can change with the addition of a single new colour.

For a constant reminder of the summer all around me, I've introduced these palettes in my home. I've picked out paint colours inspired by the palettes the seashore has produced and I've painted some old porch furniture in various shades of green and white. Using a watered-down emulsion paint, I applied layer upon layer of the colours and then roughly sanded back the paint to reveal all the different shades underneath, giving a sea-washed effect both in the colours and the textured finish.

left A mobile of sea glass, driftwood and string reflects summer sun.

right Everything about sea glass – its colour, texture and the way it reflects light – is a reminder of the seaside.

top far right The colour of sea glass translated into paint: used in multiple thin layers on furniture it will create a beautifully worn seaside effect.

below far right An old rocker, a trolley and even a galvanized tub are painted in colours inspired by the glass. Grass reeds are a natural complement as they grow in the same seaside environment.

The calendar turns and the sun-baked fields of summer become the harvest of the autumn. Colours change from bright to burning. Autumn is the cumulation of the year, what nature has been striving for: abundance. The cooler weather sends us into a whirl of activity: crops are harvested, children return to school. There's a nip in the air as we kick up our heels to squeeze every drop out of life before winter's blanket sets in. Celebrations start, city life heats up again and the social calendar will be full until the new year before you know it.

autumn

At the autumn equinox day and night are equal, life seems to get back to routine. It's time to organize the home, get your storage sorted and prepare for the busy season ahead. The palette of autumn is a sophisticated one: golden yellows blend into fiery reds, with a mix of orange in between and a crimson edge. It is this sort of palette in nature that makes the rich pattern of a paisley or the heather weave of a tweed seem so appropriate in autumn. Colours have depth – think of the faded flame-stitch pattern of a kilim rug, or the umber stripes of an Indian serape.

Touches of these fabrics will help warm the home as the season gets colder. Just as you retrieve the warmer items from your wardrobe, digging your walking boots and your waterproof jackets out of storage, so you should warm your house.

Pears are the perfect symbol of the season: everthing about them, from their rich colours to their full curvy shape, expresses the ripeness of the world at this time. First seen overflowing on a tree then plucked and enjoyed as a still life in a bowl, only next to be baked and eaten in a pie. The wonder of nature has many moments. Pumpkins and squash too have a dual life. The insides are scooped out and made into hearty soups, while the shell can be used as a decorative container to serve the soup from, or Hallowe'en lanterns filled with flickering candles.

Large wooden bowls filled with apples or nuts replace the floral decorations of summer. It is worth buying produce at a farmer's market or an organic grocer as the fruit and vegetables retain the naturally occurring variety in size, shape and colour, instead of sterile uniformity. Sadly the supermarkets see such variations as imperfections instead of nature's wonder.

Find creative ways to bring nature inside. Look to what is left in the garden. Flowers such as rudbeckia, nigella, poppies and sunflowers have wonderful sculptural seed heads, giving them a life long after what is normally considered their prime. Combine spiky thistles and plump rose hips with turning foliage for vibrant autumal displays. Dry sage in the fire place then use it to kindle the first autumnal fire – folklore has it this cleans the atmosphere, ridding your home of any negative spirits that could be lurking about! Acorns and pine cones are to autumn what pebbles and shells are to summer. Collected on woodland walks these can dot the house with rustic charm.

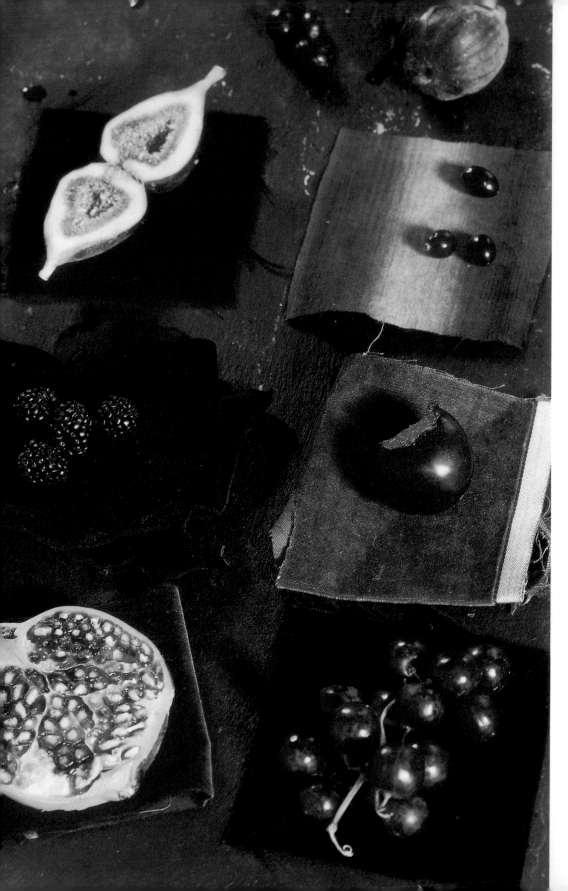

Autumn fruits

Colour plays a vital role in influencing our moods and emotions. Yellow is the colour of the sun, energizing and happy; red the colour of passion; blue evokes the seaside. With all the specialist paints available today I feel like a child in a sweet shop but a good rule is to decorate to reflect nature's pallete – nature usually gets it right. Indigenous plants and landscapes will often hold the key to which colours will work best indoors.

Try colour accents such as painting the ceiling sky blue, a Georgian tradition. If you are not bold enough to paint a whole room why not just one wall? Even the inside of a cupboard painted in a contrasting colour can make you smile each time you go to it. Or my solution to sudden colour fetishes is to paint my current favourite onto a large canvas. You can buy pre-stretched canvas in smaller sizes or make your own using stretchers from any artists' supply store, a few metres of canvas and a staple gun. Don't feel intimidated because you are painting on canvas. Apply the paint in the same way you would colour wash a wall, in thin watered down layers. When you tire of one colour simply paint it over with your new favourite.

left Seasonal fruits provide the inspiration for an autumnal colour story. **right** A large canvas is painted in tonal shades of grape, working as a backdrop to the jewel shades of the rich velvet and silk cushions covers and throw, bringing warmth to an otherwise monochrome room.

Winter comes upon us and the world is at rest again. Days are short and the weather can be dreary. We fight the elements in winter more than any other time of year. But a northern gale and grey skies make us appreciate the comforts of home all the more. Winter is the time when nature hibernates and we are not excluded. To protect yourself from harsh weather make a cosy nest for yourself and curl up in front of a crackling fire with warm woollen blankets. Drink hot chocolate and listen to soothing music while the snow falls peacefully outside.

winter

Take long candlelit baths scented with aromatic oils. Mull hot cider, infusing the room with the smell of apples and cinnamon. Activity moves indoors and this is the perfect time of year to get on with projects and crafts. Make room for these activities by designating a hobby table where materials can be kept out. Or start a project basket and keep it to hand. A jumper you are knitting not only has a better chance of being finished but also looks lovely if it is lying in a basket waiting to be picked up. If your creative endeavours are allowed to sit comfortably within a home they add to the life and spirit of a place.

When days are short compensate for the all-pervading darkness by introducing cheerful colours and uplifting patterns in your home. The Scandinavians, who have one of the harshest of winteclimates, do this so well: think of their bright checks and traditional knitting patterns. The tartans of Scotland have the same effect – warming but upbeat. A lot of the effort you put into your home in winter has to do with chasing both the cold and the blues away. Pamper yourself by surrounding yourself with tactile textures and bring out fabrics with a luxurious touch, such as velvet, thick cotton corduroy, moleskin and angora. For the ultimate cocoon wrap yourself in one of the wonderful fake furs throws that are available now (or could easily be made).

In winter the earth reveals its skeleton. Think of the wonderful sculptural form of the witch-hazel tree, how magnificent a single branch looks when brought indoors. Clipped box and bay laurel stand alone in the garden, their neat ordered shapes a somehow welcome rest for the eye after the blazing autumnal palette. Wreaths can be made from what's left in the garden, the circle signifying the completion of the year. Try making one out of twigs if no greenery is available – the barren simplicity in a room can be its own sort of poetry.

Flowers are scarce now so turn to fruit and foliage for freshening a room. Eucalyptus is said to have medicinal qualities and will last a long time: its elegance remains even when it is dried and the colour fades from green to metallic grey. Bowls of oranges and lemons can add a bright spark of colour to a room. Become an indoor gardener in winter and use this time to dream and plan your summer garden or window boxes. Mark the new year by planting an amaryllis on 1 January and enjoy its beauty at every stage as it unfolds along with the new year.

Creations

Display

A HOME SHOULD REVEAL THE PERSONALITIES OF ITS INHABITANTS. AT ITS BEST IT SHOULD BE A PORTRAIT OF WHO YOU ARE. IT IS THE SMALL TOUCHES, THE VIGNETTES WE CREATE WITH THE OBJECTS THAT HOLD MEANING TO US, THAT WILL GIVE A HOME ITS UNIQUE CHARACTER. IT IS THESE SMALL DETAILS THAT TRANSFORM A HOME INTO A PERSONAL SPACE. LOOK AT YOUR HOUSE AS AN ARTIST WOULD AND HAVE FUN CREATING VIGNETTES AS A PAINTER WOULD A STILL LIFE. Be spontaneous and use the seasons and changing light and temperature to act as prompts to reconsider the things around you. Let what's going on outside influence what happens inside your home. Rotate your favourite things from room to room to keep your home alive and in motion. Use what you already have in a different context and you'll be surprised at how stimulating your things will look when literally seen in a new light. I love scavenging mementos from nature to use within my home in fleeting still lifes. It is a way of holding onto memories of a time and place. Create tension by mixing hard and soft objects, and by placing large shapes next to small. Mix the past with the present. Punctuate something by displaying it en masse. Keep your displays revolving, and in turn your home will feel very much alive. These are the touches that will fill your house with soul and make those living within it blossom. Creativity is something we all have and it needn't be shown through the customary avenues of painting or writing; it can be as simple as the way we arrange flowers or objects on our mantel. Our surroundings hold tremendous power over our moods and emotions – use that power to positive effect.

Personal mementos

It needn't be serious artwork to hang on the wall – a collection of favourite mementoes such as postcards, children's drawings and sketches can give your home a more personal feel. Embrace the possibilities that change has to offer and create transient displays reflecting your mood and interests at the moment. Visuals will remain more spontaneous and stimulating if they are fashioned in a manner that allows for this continual influx of new ideas.

MASHOMACK POINT

MASHOMACK CREEK

S

E

1 inch = ~1/4 mile

1/8   1/4   3/8

EXPLORATION OF THE SOUL

left A laundry line strung across the wall is a great
way to hang an ever-changing array of watercolours.
above Postcards and photographs reflect the mood of a summer
holiday. **top right** Victorian seaweed prints are pinned casually to the wall,
balancing the formality of the framed picture. **centre right** Polaroids and lichen
make an intimate winter's display. **bottom right** A screen with clips nailed onto it is
the venue for a changeable show of postcards and pictures.

Florida's Beautiful Indian River

1 Start with three layers of materials. Cut the foamcore board and the batting to fit your frame. Cut the ticking 10 cm (4 in) wider all round than the foamcore.

You will need

foamcore board
polyester batting
empty frame
cotton ticking
packing tape
ribbon
map pins

2 Wrap the ticking tautly around the foamcore, sandwiching the batting between them. Tuck the corners in neatly to form a mitre , trimming the excess fabric first. Secure the ticking with small pieces of tape.

3 To attach the ribbon in a diagonal pattern, work from the front of the board. Secure the pieces at each end on the edge of the board with map pins, pulling them taut and allowing enough ribbon to overlap to the back of the board.

4 When you are happy that the ribbons are evenly spaced wrap the ends around to the back of the board and secure them with small pieces of tape. Then remove the map pins from the edge of the board and insert them into the front of the board at the points where the ribbons cross., pushing them all the way in.

5 Push the completed board into the frame, and finish it with packing tape, making sure you seal the raw edges of the ticking and the ribbon.

Notice board

At last a stylish bulletin board that will look as good in your sitting room as in a home office. The frame, found in a junk shop, is made out of old pine moulding. It's been painted with layers of emulsion in varying shades of white for a mellowed look. Old family photos and personal mementos can be tucked throughout the ribbons without damage from pins, and layered and changed as new favourites arrive.

Transitory displays

Hanging paintings on unyielding walls can be an intimidating project. You have to be sure that you are not going to change your mind too soon, because once you have banged nails into the walls changing their position can be difficult. To answer this problem I've devised a display wall in my home using narrow shelves about 8 cm (3 in) wide. Here I prop an ever-changing variety of sketches and photos. By the same principle, you could hang a single big painting above your mantelpiece and then layer smaller pieces in front of it by simply leaning them against the others. This allows you freedom to add an inspiring postcard or a new favourite photo to the display when the mood strikes.

left It doesn't have to be art for you to hang it on the walls. If you cannot afford original artworks your walls don't have to go bare. Try hanging quilts, clothing or textiles, or even a collection of hats, as here. Garden chairs and a flower pot borrowed from the garden add to the breezy summery feel suggested by a collection of straw hats.
right Alcove shelving continued across a chimney breast makes a perch for an ever-changing exhibition.

Make the everyday beautiful

You don't need to surround yourself with a host of material possessions in order to create a beautiful home – instead make the everyday beautiful. By giving thought to the objects we hold and use in our daily rituals you can make these mundane routines more pleasurable. There is an appealing honesty to hand-crafted objects that are designed with simplicity and function in mind. Another bonus is they don't beg to be hidden away when not in use. A vintage watering can or tin dust-pan and wooden-handled brush will not scream out at you in a room like modern plastic versions would. Often, too, these things don't cost any more than their mass-produced equivalents would. Look around you at the objects you use constantly: kitchen utensils, pots and pans, coat hangers, even scrubbing brushes. With some thought all these things can be a pleasure to the hand as well as the eye.

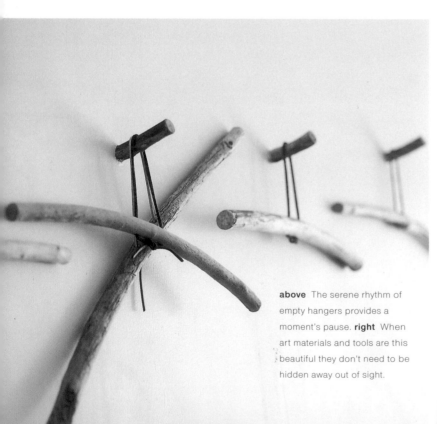

above The serene rhythm of empty hangers provides a moment's pause. **right** When art materials and tools are this beautiful they don't need to be hidden away out of sight.

Remember how as a child in school you would take in contributions to the class nature table? Recreate this idea in your home to add vitality and energy to a room. As it is usually the focal point in a room, a mantelshelf is the perfect place to display an array of finds that

a home is not a static place

change as often as the weather does. Try a row of pine cones graduating in size and watch them open in the warmth; a pile of pebbles from a coastal walk grouped according to colour; or a plain white jug filled with cow parsley from the hedgerows.

Display can be a form of visual poetry. **above, left to right** A sketch taped casually on the wall allows for easy changes. Straw textures accentuate a summery mood. Rocks from a summer's holiday are sorted and labelled, holding memories of a time and place in a jar. **below, left to right** Stones collected on the beach are gilded with hearts. A single apple

plucked from an orchard on a weekend walk is as beautiful as any object of art. Twigs from the same walk create a natural sculpture that can be enjoyed and then changed as the seasons evolves. **opposite** A large cloud painting on an unframed canvas simply pinned on the wall serves as a backdrop for a layering of seasonal mantel displays

Painted cupboard

You will need

wooden cupboard

sandpaper

cotton rag

3 tins emulsion paint in 3 different shades of creamy white, ranging from a pale to a dark tone

3 large plastic buckets

mixing stick

water

9 cm (3 in) paintbrush

1 cm (½ in) flat paint brush

pencil

clear acrylic varnish

varnish brush

Junk shops are great places to scout for inexpensive furniture. Look for pieces with good proportions and clean simple lines. Many of the things on offer can easily be transformed with this simple paint technique. The technique uses water-based paint so it is easy to do with a minumum of fuss and no chemicals. A broad flat space is the perfect place to put a favourite motif, such as the dove I've painted here.

1 To prepare the cupboard, lightly sand it then wipe it with a damp rag. Using the mid tone paint, apply a first coat over the entire surface. When this has dried you can apply thinner layers of paint. Mix the darkest shade with 3 parts paint to 1 part water and then apply it thinly to the panel sections of the cupboard, brushing in the direction of the wood grain. Dilute the palest paint in the same way and apply it to the frame surrounding the panels. Allow to dry.

2 Dilute the mid-toned paint and apply it over the entire cupboard again. Repeat this layering process 3 times, allowing each coat to dry before applying the next. Finish with the separate coats of dark and light paints. Roughly sand the cabinet, working in the direction of the wood grain. As you sand you will reveal the different layers of paint to create a soft graduated tonal effect. At this stage you can if you wish apply further layers or even a final coat of very thin paint diluted 1 part paint to 1 part water.

3 Enlarge the template of the dove to your required size and using a pencil trace it onto the cabinet door.

4 Using the artist's brush and the lightest colour, paint in the body of the bird. Apply the paint in short strokes, twisting the brush at the end to create the effect of feathers. Using longer strokes paint the tail and wings, following the direction of the feathers. On the wings, paint the longer under feathers first and then the shorter top ones over the top. The paint may dry out and become slightly powdery, but this will help to create a raised, three-dimensional image.

5 When the dove is dry, apply two coats of acrylic varnish to the entire cupboard to seal the surface.

Watch as the year blossoms

Flowers and foliage add life to a room. I used to spend a fortune on fresh cut flowers but now I've realised that with a bit of ingenuity I can make my own arrangements from what is available in my small garden. I like to use indigenous flowers and foliage rather than exotic imports as this secures a sense of place, and seasonal blooms help to ground you in the revolution of the year. In spring I become an indoor gardener, indulging myself with the delight of forcing bulbs. A tub of Paperwhites can usher in spring long before the weather does. In the autumn I turn to berries, rosehips and seasonal foliage. Small posies can have as much impact as larger displays with some thought to their placement. Think of the places you go to during your daily routine, such as your bathroom sink. A small posy here will cheer you when you wake up in the morning and again before you go to bed at night.

Floral displays don't have to be over-stuffed vases. A small simple gesture is often enough to act as a reminder of what is happening outdoors. Single flowers look great in milk bottles or bigger bouquets in kitchen storage jars. Don't be afraid to place humble containers such as these on your most elegant dining table – it's the mix that makes it fun.

Flower mirror

Mirrors provide wonderful opportunites for small decorative gestures because our daily routine ensures that we look into them at least once a day. Pressing hydrangrea flowers between glass preserves their fragile beauty, carrying the feel of summer throughout the year The colours will fade gradually, but this will merely add to their muted charm. A backless frame holding two sheets of glass (opposite page) can act as a showcase for the seasons. Fill it with a succession of flowers and foliage, from the delicate fronds of evergreen ferns in winter to vibrant orange nasturtium flowers in summer, spidery maple leaves in autumn and simple violets in spring.

You will need

fresh flowers for border
blotting paper
I piece of picture frame glass, cut to size
I piece of mirror glass, cut to size
double-sided tape
heavy-duty adhesive linen tape
ribbon

I Press individual fresh flower heads between sheets of blotting paper. Place them in a large book and stack other heavy books on top. Leave them for at least 3 weeks to dry out completely.

2 Have a piece of picture frame glass and a piece of mirror glass cut to the size you want. Ask your glazier to make 2 holes at the top of each piece, 3.5 cm (1 ½ in) from the edge and 5cm (2 in) apart.

3 Cut small pieces of double-sided tape and stick them to the back of each flower. Lay the mirror flat and stick the fowers evenly around the edge.

4 Carefully lay the glass on top of the mirror to seal in the flowers and then tape each corner diagonally using the heavy-duty tape to secure the glass.

5 To hang the mirror, thread the ribbon through the 2 holes and tie it in a bow.

Soft furnishings

I HAVE A PASSION FOR TEXTILES. TO ME, CHANGING FABRICS IS ONE OF THE EASIEST WAYS TO REINVENT A ROOM. A BED, CHAIR, TABLE OR SOFA CAN AND SHOULD CHANGE FROM WINTER TO SUMMER. BY CHANGING SLIPCOVERS, CURTAINS, TABLE CLOTHS, BED LINEN, CUSHION COVERS, OR JUST THROWING A PIECE OF FABRIC OVER A SIDE TABLE, YOU CAN IN ONE STROKE CHANGE THE ATMOSPHERE OF A ROOM. Think of it as creating wardrobes for your home! Slipcovers can be a bold way to achieve a quick changeover. Even a couple of side chairs in different guises can punctuate the seasonal mood of a room. Or transform your sofa with a paisley shawl and change of cushion covers. I have a small collection of throws I use just for this purpose. Ever useful, a throw can reinvent itself as a tablecloth, a bed throw, or even an *ad hoc* curtain. They add instant texture and are a way to add colour or pattern to a room without making a long-term or expensive commitment. Make seasonal nests for yourself: in winter throw a fake fur blanket in front of the fire and snuggle up with a cup of hot chocolate. A summer hammock can be strewn with cushions made from vintage prints for extra comfort. The wonderful thing about fabrics is they need not be permanent; you can be a bit more adventurous with pattern and colour as they can be revolved so easily around the house and throughout the year. Layer and unlayer as the weather dictates.

Summer shirting

Don't limit yourself to furnishing fabrics when you are looking for ideas for your home. Fashion fabrics used out of context can often be much less expensive and add a certain whimsy to a room. Here, inspiration for a number of decorating ideas is found in a classic man's formal striped shirt. It adds the same crisp clean freshness to a room that it does to a wardrobe.

Buy a few metres in a combination of co-ordinating stripes and have fun making pillow cases, laundry bags, even duvet covers. Quilting is an excellent way of using up fabric scraps and today with machine sewing it needn't be the tedious labour-intensive chore it once was. Trimmings such as ribbons and buttons can be found in abundance at antique markets.

Second-hand clothing can be a springboard for inspiration. Men's night-shirts from the early part of the century often have beautiful mellowed stripes and women's dirndl skirts from the 1950s can have amusing, slightly kitsch, conversational·prints that work well on flat surfaces such as roller blinds or cushions, so that you can appreciate the large-scale design. Worn-out denims and canvas can be cut into patches and stitched together to cover a footrest; the fabric will still be sturdy enough to take lots of wear and tear.

Look to your closet for the things you don't wear any more. Maybe the style or size doesn't suit any more, but you have been hanging on to it because you still like the fabric. There's a whole treasure of goodies tucked away in your wardrobe.

right Summer shirting sparks off an array of decorating ideas in the bedroom – from the patchwork quilt displayed on the wall to the checked pillow sham. The duvet cover is made from sections of shirting pieced together. **far right** Drawstring laundry and storage bags are made from shirting fabric trimmed with contrasting grosgrain ribbon.

Autumnal Throw

Patchwork is one of the thriftiest ways of using up fabric scraps. It's a technique our grandmothers used and for good reason. This fireside throw is made of odd pieces of tweed combined with a luxurious velvet trim and lambswool backing. It is sturdy enough to be thrown on the floor yet welcoming enough to snuggle into.

You will need
assorted pieces of tweed to cut into scraps
cotton velvet for the border
thread
lambswool

1 Cut squares out of the tweed fabrics. The ideal size is about 10 cm (4 in) square. Sew 10 squares together to form a long strip. Make another 12 strips in the same way so that you have 13 in total, and then sew the strips together. Press the seams open flat.

2 For the border, cut 2 pieces of velvet 20 cm (8 in) wide and 20 cm (8 in) longer than the tweed panel, and 2 pieces 20 cm (8 in) wider than the panel and 20 cm (8 in) long. Right sides facing, join one short piece to one long piece. Make a triangle by folding the corners in. Sew along this line, trim the excess fabric and press the seams open. Join all 4 pieces in this way to make the border.

3 With the border wrong sides out, pin the tweed panel to one side of the border, right sides together and pin, baste and sew around all 4 sides.

4 Cut the lambswool to the same size as the tweed panel and pin this to the back opening, right sides together. Sew around 3 sides, leaving the other side open. Press the seams open and turn the throw right side out through the open side. Slipstitch the opening closed and each corner of the back panel at the inside edge to secure.

Using everyday objects

You do not have to spend a fortune decorating your home with shop-bought soft furnishings — basic household items can be an endless source of inspiration. To me, one of the simple pleasures of life is the humble tea towel. Its clean fresh checks and stripes makes me think of spring all year long. Collect different ones and sew them into various shapes and guises: they can be transformed into curtains, a patchwork for a table cloth, be turned into cushion covers or simply hung for use on a wall. New ones look fresh and bright, but old ones have their own faded charm too. Try scouting antique markets. Old French linen tea towels are especially beautiful.

far left Nothing could be simpler than using heavy cotton tea towels to cover the seat pads of wooden chairs. **left** A variety of old and new tea towels make for refreshing cushion covers. **above** A soft Roman blind made from a blue-and-white checked tea towel print lends a spring feel all year. **above right** Necessity makes for clean living: hung in a row these towels make a practical and pretty display. **right** Half a vintage tablecloth becomes a café curtain.

Sailor pillow

You will need

an adult-size sailor top – look in antique markets and second-hand shops

thread

I love vintage clothing and I incorporate pieces into my home as display. Often you find garments that are damaged and so sold cheaply. But that needn't hinder you: with careful cutting you can salvage the good bits and make up small accessories.

1 Cut three pieces from the sailor top. Cut a rectangular section from the collar, and cut one piece from the back and a longer piece from the front, as indicated in the diagram. Cut each piece 2.5 cm (1 in) wider than the collar to allow for the seams. The back piece should be equal in length to the collar and the front piece. Add 2.5 cm (1 in) seam allowance to the length on the back and front pieces. Remove the sleeve patch, the pocket and the necktie from the top and retain them.

2 On the front piece, turn in a double hem along one of the short sides onto the right side. Attach the collar to the front piece by stitching along the top of the hemmed edge, keeping the hemmed edge visible.

3 Sew the patch to the pocket and then sew the pocket onto the centre of the front of the pillow. Make 2 buttonholes on the collar section, 1 cm (½ in) apart and wide enough for the necktie.

4 With right sides together, sew the back and front pieces along three sides, but do not sew the collar. Turn right side out, then topstitch the collar in place.

5 Thread the necktie through the butonholes and tie it in a bow. To secure it, slipstitch it in place with a few stitches at the back of the buttonhole.

Button lampshade

Here's an idea for buying something ready made and then personalizing it. After looking for lampshades for my home I became discouraged, mainly by the outrageous prices. So I turned to the local department store and bought the simplest, most inexpensive shades I could find, then sat myself down for an hour in the sun and used ribbons and vintage buttons to create something a bit more special. And when you haven't splashed out a huge amount of money you will change your lampshades more frequently!

You will need
a plain shop-bought lampshade
ribbon for trim
approximately 10 pearl buttons
all-purpose glue
double-sided sellotape

1 To work out how much ribbon you need, wrap it around the top and bottom of the lampshade, adding 1 cm (½in) for the overlap. Lay the ribbon flat and spread an even amount of glue onto the back of the ribbon. Carefully stick the ribbon to the lampshade, lining up the overlap with the seam of the lampshade and tucking under the raw edges.

2 Stick small pieces of double-sided tape on the back of the buttons and place them on the lampshade, adjusting them as necessary. When you are happy with the arrangement, mark the position of each button with a pencil, remove the tape from the buttons and glue them firmly in place.

Use cushion covers as accessories; change them to suit your mood and the atmosphere you want to create. Make them out of old fabric remnants or try designer sales for end of rolls sold cheaply. Use bandanas or tie a scarf around a cushion for a quick fix. I have one big wicker chair that I call my seasonal chair. I change the seat cushion by tucking different fabrics around it and switch throw cushions every once in a while. It is the first thing I see when I walk into my living room and it's always a welcoming note.

Decorating cushions

Daisy tablecloth

Even the most unsightly table can be transformed with the throw of a cloth. Here my husband's old workbench reinvents itself as a side board. I don't like spending hours of time on these projects so I used a machine zig-zag stitch for the appliqué and saved hours of labour.

You will need

medium-weight artist's canvas (you can find this at most good art shops)
similar weight white linen
pencil
thread
4 large buttons (I've used antique ones)

1 Wash the artist's canvas to pre-shrink it and allow it to dry. It has a tendency to crack and have a rumpled look after washing, which adds to the character of the fabric. Measure the table you wish to cover and cut pieces for the top and back, allowing 2.5 cm (1 in) all around each piece for seam allowance. The front and side panels should ideally be cut from one long piece of fabric and you should allow an extra 20 cm (8 in) added to the seam allowance for each of

the two box pleats at the front corners. If you do need to join lengths of canvas to make the front and side piece position the seams so that they will be hidden in the corner pleats.

2 Pre-wash the linen. Measure the bottom edge of the front and side pieces and cut a piece of linen to this length and 30 cm (12 in) deep. Again, if you need to join lengths, hide the seams in the box pleat. To make the border, mark equal distances along the the top edge for the peaks, then mark the distance half way between each of these marks 10 cm (4 in) below the first row of marks for the valleys. Cut from dot to dot to form the zigzag.

4 To make the corner pleats fold in 5 cm (2 in) on either side, so that the total width of the pleat is 10 cm (4 in). Pin the pleat in place and make sure the centre

3 Sew the border to the bottom of the front and sides section of the table cloth, with the right side of the border facing the wrong side of the cloth. Then flip the border up to hide the seam and pin it in place. Sew along the edge of the zigzags using a very narrow zigzag stitch to attach the border to the cloth, and then press.

lines up with one corner of the table. Make a second pleat for the other front corner, adjusting the first pleat if necessary. Press the pleats then sew them in place 1 cm (½ in) below the upper edge.

5 Cut petal shapes from the white linen and pin them in place on the front of the cloth, then sew them using a small zigzag stitch. Sew a button to the centre of each flower. To assemble the tablecloth, hem the bottom long edge of the back panel, and then sew the pieces together as shown in step 1. Press open the seams, clip the corners and turn right side out.

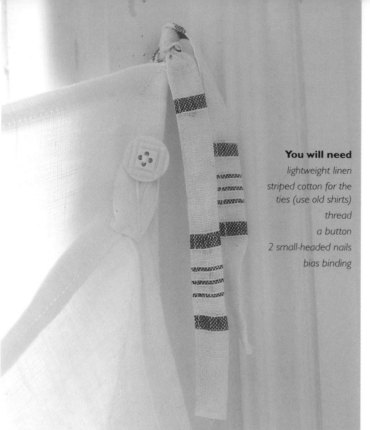

You will need

lightweight linen
striped cotton for the
ties (use old shirts)
thread
a button
2 small-headed nails
bias binding

Summer curtain

Sheer white café curtains are a great way to add privacy without blocking a view or the light. Here is proof that so often the simplest ideas are the best. Take short cuts with sewing where you can – for instance if the fabric has an attractive selvage incorporate it into the design it and save yourself time on hemming.

1 Measure the area of the window you want to cover, and take the dimensions of the curtain from that, adding 2.5 cm (1 in) all round for the hems. Cut the linen and turn under a double hem on all 4 sides.

2 For the ties, cut 2 pieces of cotton 40 cm (16 in) long by 4.5 cm (1¾ in) wide. Press under 1 cm (½ in) all round, press in half lengthwise and sew around the 3 open sides.

3 Sew the ties to the top corners of the curtain, placing them diagonally across the corners.

4 Make a loop from the bias binding and sew it onto the wrong side of the lower left corner of the curtain.

5 Sew a button 3.5 cm (1 ½ in) below the right tie. To hang the curtain hammer a nail either side of the window frame and knot the ties on the nails. To fold back the curtain fix the loop on the button.

Living spaces

Relaxing

THE LIVING ROOM IS USUALLY THE FIRST ROOM YOU SEE WHEN YOU WALK INTO A HOUSE — IT IS THE ROOM THAT WELCOMES YOU HOME. BUT IT IS A PUBLIC ROOM AS WELL AS A PRIVATE ONE, AND SO IT IS VERY EASY TO SLIP INTO THE TRADITION OF MAKING THIS ROOM THE MOST FORMAL IN A HOUSE. PERSONAL TOUCHES ARE OFTEN RESERVED FOR OTHER ROOMS SUCH AS BEDROOMS. But this can lend a stiff welcome. A house should reveal its inhabitants slowly, drawing a visitor in. A living room that is inviting and lived in can bring a warm welcome to you and guests each time they come through the door, making you and them feel much more at home. Try breaking down the space between private and public, mixing formal pieces with more informal whimsical touches that make a house a home. Simple ideas can have a big impact. and rooms that change with the calendar year make a home that houses your soul and not just your body. I learned a good lesson recently: I realized that the room in my house I felt most at home in was my top-floor studio. It is filled with sketches and photos casually pinned up on the wall, and an array of objects of personal meaning and inspiration that is constantly changing. In contrast, I would keep my living room clean and more guarded. I wasn't living in it but saving it for special occasions, and I found when I brought people into the room it didn't say anything about me. Then I thought why not treat this room as an extension of myself, as my studio naturally is? Why not make my living space as alive as I do my 'designated' creative environment? A living room should be just that: a room to live in.

The mood of a room will change as the seasons do. I think the first view one sees when walking into a room is the most important and that means giving the room a focal point. If you are lucky enough to have a big fireplace this will inevitably become the focus in winter. Even if it is not a working one it can be filled with candles to create the illusion of the glow of firelight. In the summer daylight becomes more important so the windows naturally receive more attention. Replace your heavy winter curtains with a more lightweight sheer fabric and move the furniture around so that the window is easily accessible for opening and closing, allowing the summer sunshine to pour in.

A city loft with a soft touch celebrates the changing seasons. **left** An open-plan space is divided off with drapes that change from a rich dark brown to a sheer white cotton. A moveable screen is used to focus attention on the dining area, creating a more intimate space for a winter dinner party. **right** The drama of an over-scaled quince blossom ushers in the arrival of spring. **far right, from top** A patchwork of vintage tea towels makes a refreshingly different tablecloth. The mantelpiece gives this small area a focus and serves as a useful display area. Stretching a fabric panel across a fireplace when it is not in use is an effective way of shifting emphasis from what is an empty space for part of the year.

above Think of cushion covers as accessories for the home; they are the perfect venue for using daring prints as they can be changed so easily. A faux leopard print adds a dramatic touch, accenting this chair in winter. **below** Tableware need not be matching. An eclectic mix of candles and glasses adds a personal touch. Elegant white roses complement the look beautifully.

This romantic love nest is a charming alternative to the standard couch and two chairs seating arrangement. It is made simply by hanging curtains off a rod that is suspended from the ceiling. A single size mattress is placed on a plywood base and covered with fabric; this sets the stage for an endless combination of textures and materials. **left** Winter is the time when we seem to dress up the home. Dramatic velvet curtains and bed dressing in bottle green set a glamorous scene. Mirrors can be used to open up a space and reflect light back into the room. **right** In spring a softer mood is conjured up with drapes of the palest sky blue and light layers of white bed linens covering the daybed. The wrought iron table has been moved for the season to another setting and is replaced by a small folding garden table. **below** Flowers have a beauty at each stage in their lives, like these spring peonies whose falling petals only add to their charm.

Change is the only constant. Satisfy your senses and follow your instincts: when it is rainy and cold our instincts tell us to stay indoors and create nests; when it is warm and sunny we are itching to go outside or to open the windows and let the outside in. Bring in symbols of the season as temporary displays in your home. Then go beyond those symbols and ask yourself how you respond emotionally to each season, how the light, weather and colours of each season make you feel. Satisfy these needs through changes in your physical environment.

How you feel today probably isn't the same as how you felt last year or even last week. So alter your rooms with your moods.

A spacious, soothing white room enjoys a nocturnal play of light and shadow in winter. **above left** Piles of cushions are scattered in front of a roaring hearth, making an inviting seasonal nest. **above centre** An exotic atmosphere is created in winter using Turkish and Afghanistan textiles to drape the large white sofa, accented by black velvet roses, the glow of candlelight and the scent of incense. **above** A deep pile of traditional knits from a mix of cultures is kept close at hand, as much for aesthetic as for practical reasons.

Keep your house alive and in motion; introduce objects that reflect your newest interests. A row of postcards propped on the mantel against a more formal oil painting can vary seasonally. The painting will probably stay in its place but with different accents it will add freshness to a room. Your friends will be delighted with the visual stimulus each time they come over. Gather objects around you that hold memories of places or people who have been in your life, or use things from other areas of the house. A row of enamel jugs usually kept in the kitchen can make a nice surprise as a temporary display on a living room sidetable. The idea is to use what you already have in different ways.

above left In summer the room is kept spare and open – light floods in through bare windows, allowing a large gardenia plant to flourish. The floor is cleared of rugs to reveal the clear honey-like tones of the floorboards. Draped in its summer dressings, the sofa is brought forward into the room to make the most of the natural light. **above** Variously textured white and ivory embroidered linen and heavily slubbed fringed cotton blankets and rugs work as warm weather throws and cushion covers.

If you start with the main pieces of furniture, which in a living room will probably be seating, and then work towards the details, you will be able to put a room together that has a clean base with which you can then play to add seasonal details. The key is to have a versatile base that leaves room for possibilities.

The most important thing about living areas is to have comfort for your lifestyle. It is worth investing money in good comfortable seating, or the time into tracking these down at second-hand markets. These are the pieces that will form the skeleton of the room, so choose

above left Light, colour and space give this room a springtime feel. Colours inspired by the freshest buds carry on the atmosphere. **above centre** A chair gets a change of clothing when the mood strikes. Inexpensive straw shopping baskets work effectively as movable storage. **above right** A plain woollen blanket is personalized with velvet and silk ribbon. **below left** Flowers soften the edges of a room.

below centre White floorboards and bare walls reflect light and emphasize the open space. Basic wooden trays planted with Paperwhites are all that is needed to add fragrance, colour and a flash of beauty. **below right** Plain white china plates look best on a simple trestle table painted primrose yellow. **opposite** Glass vases in varying sizes are treated like sculpture, making a rhythmic dance along the mantelpiece.

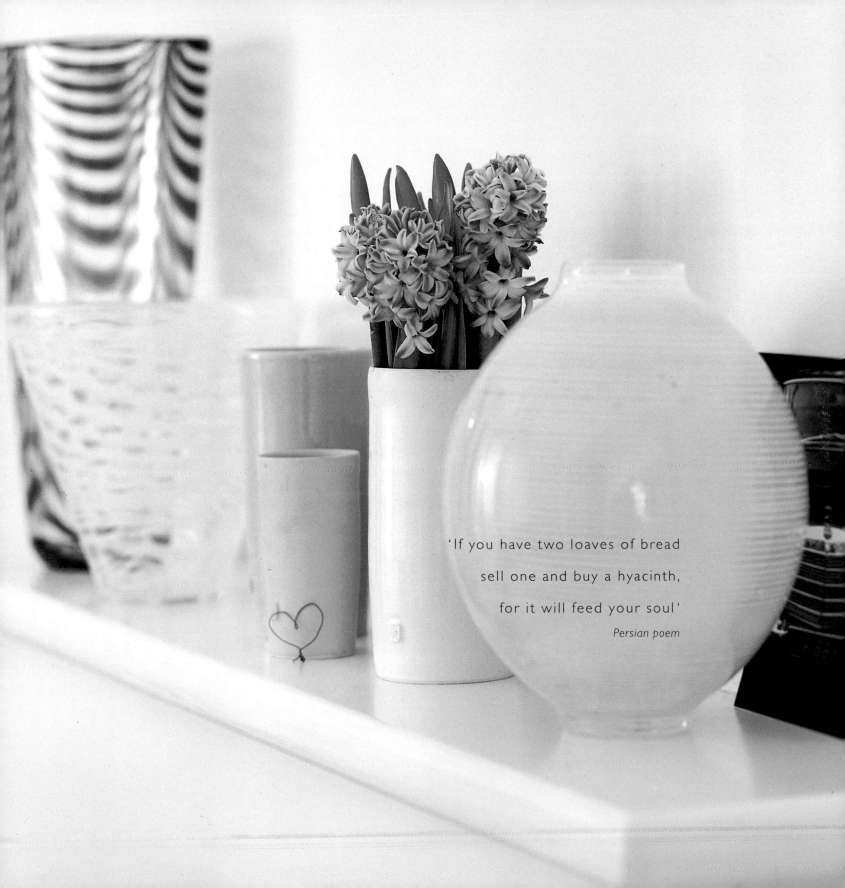

'If you have two loaves of bread

sell one and buy a hyacinth,

for it will feed your soul'

Persian poem

carefully. Nothing can beat a big comfortable couch and chairs slipcovered in white or off-white fabric. Think of your lifestyle: perhaps the standard three-piece suite isn't for you. Unconventional seating arrangements, such as a collection of odd armchairs or scattered floor cushions around a low table, could make you more comfortable. A daybed can be a romantic substitute for a sofa and it also serves as a guest bed when needed. This can be dressed and undressed as the seasons change. The key is to keep these investment pieces simple and classic, something you can live with for a long time, with seasonal adaptations such as throws and pillows layered on top.

Furniture should be easygoing in care and up-keep – slipcovers should be made from pre-washed fabric so they can be regularly thrown in the washing machine for easy cleaning. If you feel relaxed about your home, others will pick up the cue and feel comfortable also.

After the seating is established look at the table space. The coffee table has become a much-loved necessity in today's lifestyle, holding drinks and flowers, and serving as a central point around which to sit. Try placing a long bench in front of your couch to stack books and a tray of tea on. It should be sturdy enough to withstand the odd pair of feet – nothing in your home should be so precious that you can't

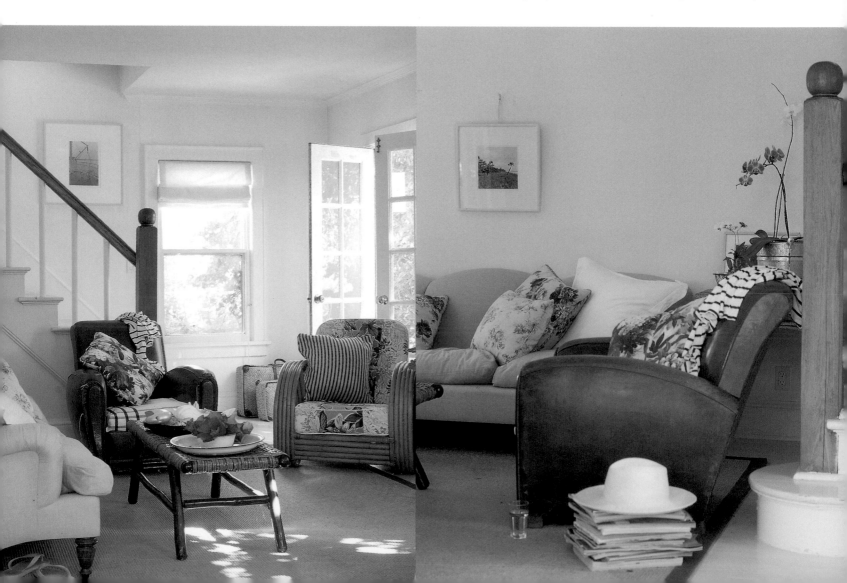

kick off your shoes and rest your feet on top of it! Side tables can be picked up at flea markets; just look for great shapes that can be easily freshened up with a coat of paint. Or try stacking a pile of big art books on top of each other with a small tray on top – this can serve as a temporary side table, a convenient place to rest a glass. All these *ad hoc* ideas add a certain flexibility and give you the freedom to alter the movement of a room.

So often these days our rooms have to serve a multitude of purposes. My living room became a much friendlier place when I accepted the fact that a corner of it had to function as an office also.

far left A holiday home immediately says summer with a playful mix of pattern. **centre left** Even a robust leather chair goes on vacation – strewn with floral cushions and a vintage tablecloth it is more comfortable for summer's bare legs. **centre right** A flash of colour comes from a glorious bunch of hibiscus floating in an enamel bowl. **below** Blur the definition between inside and out with doors flung wide open and the use of outside patio furniture and plants indoors.

Instead of hiding the fact I now celebrate it, and the feeling of industry this area generates, with notes and messages pinned on the wall, adds a wonderful life to this room. The function of our rooms changes from day to night as well as seasonally. Take note of this and make sure your furniture is as flexible as your lifestyle and use the room accordingly. Keep your furniture portable and move it as the seasons change, pulling it closer to the fire in winter and leaving things more open and spare in summer. Folding tables and chairs help to make a home more flexible. Try scouting out some of the wonderful old tables from the 1930s and '40s at flea markets or use old folding garden chairs for additional seating when needed. They can be shifted around to change the function of a room as your needs change. In an open-plan space a screen is a great way to make an area more intimate and it can be moved around to disguise areas of clutter.

For flooring, my favourite treatment is always bare floorboards, whether they are painted, colourwashed to a pale limed effect or stained to bring out the natural effect of the wood. They require a minimum of upkeep, complement almost any decorating style, and they are versatile enough to adapt to differing climatic conditions. Large throw rugs can be used to add warmth in winter, and then rolled away or used as table throws in summer.

Making the transition from warm weather to cool, the subtle change in colour and texture from white cotton sheeting to heavier natural unbleached linen slipcovers sets the stage for a changing season. **far left** Windows thrown open and a spray of delicate yellow tulips evoke sunshine. **left** The pleasure of colour and texture stimulates the senses. **opposite** While the backdrop remains constant the details of this room gently evolve from one season to the next: the collection of cushion covers becomes deeper in tone as the seasons progress and the vase holds winter foliage.

above Signs of seasonal change are indicated by your wardrobe – when you put away your winter coat and replace it with a lightweight mackintosh to ward off spring rain you know it is time to freshen your home also. **right and opposite** Accents direct the focus from one season to the next, with the use of lighter colours for spring and deeper ones for the autumn. All-season evergreen plants such as the sculptural clipped box look stylish potted in utilitarian galvanized buckets purchased from a local hardware shop. **top far right** Throws are the quickest way to warm a room and add a flash of seasonal colour. **far right** A dramatic over-scaled ceramic bowl generously filled with walnuts and placed directly on the floor creates a sense of abundance.

Playful vignettes incite curiosity
and invite the eye to wander

Once the basics are established accessories can be changed as your moods and needs require. Textiles are my primary way of adding seasonal interest. Cushions are comparable to jewellery: small details that lift an overall look. And as they take only a small amount of fabric they are relatively inexpensive. You can use bolder fabrics and colours

above from left Antique ticking dresses a chair for winter. Ideas can be as impromptu as this drummer boy's jacket enlivened with a sprig from the garden. The last of the rose hips make an amusing still life. **below from left** The open-weave of this linen makes a

charming slipcover. Look to unusual places for inspiration: this cover is actually a bath towel but it is perfectly at home on a pillow. Enamel dishes hold a collection of seaside mementos. **opposite** Throw cushions in knitted wool covers create a cosy winter nest.

without fear, for when you tire of them they can be switched around and easily stored away until the next time. You can get away with using less-than-perfect remnants that are sold at a more reasonable price and just cut the fabric to hide any flaws. I also love collecting old textiles from markets and fashioning them into cushion covers.

Mixing and matching patterns can be fun. A standard ticking stripe looks fresh in spring layered next to a faded floral cushion, but can work just as well in cold weather mixed with a rich paisley design. Throws are another way to instantly alter the mood of a room; I have a stack of blankets, rugs and bedcovers I keep just for this purpose. Don't forget to look in your wardrobe for inspiration also. My velvet evening wrap lives on a big comfortable chair in the winter months. and in the summer a pretty crocheted shawl comes out of my closet to grace an ottoman. Try tucking a few metres of fabric around a seat cushion — use tweed for colour and warmth in the winter or try a gingham tablecloth in the same way for spring. A leather armchair can be covered with a voluminous old linen sheet to lighten the look for summer — don't worry about making a perfect set of fitted slipcovers, just knot the corners at the side. Or cover a small wooden side chair in a succession of different fabrics so it becomes an accent in a room, complementing the seasons.

far left In autumn, as the days slowly become chillier and light levels fall, gradually introduce warmer fabrics. Cushions covered in cashmere have the same comforting appeal as an old cardigan. **centre left** The myriad colours offered by the autumnal palette of turning leaves are always an inspiration. **centre right** Throws like this deeply fringed chocolate shawl are both a stylish and versatile way to add warmth and colour to a room. The softly quilted cream cotton slipcovers on the sofa and ottoman are a perfect base for changing layers of seasonal dressing. **right** A generously proportioned bowl filled with windfall apples is both inviting and tempting.

Collections of textiles that are recycled for seasonal change in this way don't have to be put into hibernation and hidden away when they are not in use. Folded into neat piles and tied up with linen tape or brightly coloured ribbon they can make satisfying bundles that are attractive

Make space to contemplate the beauty of nature

enough to be displayed on book shelves or stacked in a corner against the wall. Or pack them into wicker baskets that can also serve as side tables. This way they can still be enjoyed all year round as part of the decoration of your home, and they are a visible reminder to you to maintain a constant injection of new textures and colours to prevent the room from becoming static and dull.

opposite An enclosed porch is perfectly balanced between indoors and out. **above, from left** Take advantage of glorious views by positioning furniture to invite peaceful contemplation. Enjoy seasonal wonders outdoors, then bring individual finds home. **below from left** A stove extends the use of this room into winter. Savour still lifes such as the wonderful colours of herbal tea or a pile of logs.

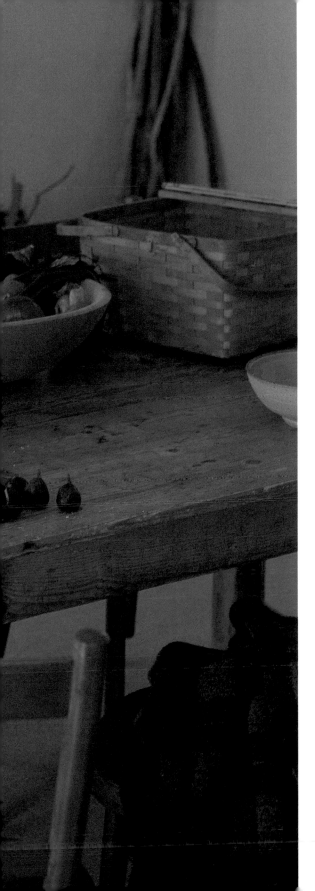

Gathering and entertaining

So many of our traditional yearly celebrations revolve around the preparation of food. These festivals play an important role in marking the calendar year and highlighting the different qualities each season brings. They add a certain structure to our lives, keeping us in tune with the rhythms of nature. Although our supermarket shelves carry produce that has been flown in from other climates all over the globe, the cycles of scarcity and then abundance of fresh produce as it comes into its true season is still exciting. The first taste of fresh strawberries heralds the summer sun to come, and piles of jewel-like tangerines, lemons and limes cheer the winter months. The dining area is where you open your home to your friends, to the people you care to share your life with. It is a place for meeting and for conversation. A table should be conducive not just to beauty but to a discourse of ideas. Food, the way it is served, and the atmosphere in which it is served, is all part of this hospitality. It's a way of giving and allowing people to come into your life. The style in which you do this counts; it is a reflection of who you are. Your style sets the tone not just for a pretty table but for so much more.

Just as the year has a rhythm of seasons so does a day and the atmosphere of a space will subtly change as both the day and the seasons unfold. The dining table plays a role that is central to the rhythm of a home. Where one day there are tears falling in a cup of tea, on another occasion in that same spot will be laughter. Just as nature has seasons and moods so too do we. And my kitchen table has seen it all. What laughter, tears, love and just about every other emotion one could imagine, has taken place around that table. We eat, celebrate holidays, entertain, do homework, cook, gossip, unpack groceries, linger over cups of tea, paint, pay bills. It's polished with beeswax and scrubbed down with soap; covered one hour in sticky jam, the next in homework and later still is glowing in candlelight ready for an evening meal. The duality of this space is fascinating; it is an immediate reflection of the range of emotions and moods that a home harbours. In turn the physical space needs to be fluid, flexible and open to spontaneity to happily accommodate this multiplicity of emotions.

One of the greatest inspirations for freshening your home is arriving home with an armload of groceries and flowers fresh from the market. There is something so fundamental about the weekly renewal of food supplies in the home, about feeding a family or sharing food with friends. It is an age-old ritual – not just a chore but a way of

Gathering and entertaining

A few bold gestures mark the season. A disused fireplace doubles as a stage set for seasonal vignettes. **far right** For winter it is filled with church candles surrounded by twigs collected on a weekend walk. The large bunch of mistletoe hangs above as a symbol of the season. The home-made chair covers are a pretty touch, contrasting nicely with the coolness of the room. **right** A summer landscape is layered with quick watercolour studies painted of the sky each weekend over the summer months. A toy boat from childhood stays in use as a memento of summers past. **below** African daisies in galvanized pots hanging on a blank wall bring nature closer to the window and enliven the view.

showing your love. The colours of the changing seasons bring life to the room. My kitchen table has become the place of honour where I routinely place a small still life of natural objects. It could be as plain as a mixing bowl filled with nectarines or a jug overflowing with wild flowers. Maybe it is only noticed at a glance, but hopefully it serves as a point for those who pass to stop, look and, if only briefly, think 'oh, how beautiful'. It is a small gesture, but who knows the value of a moment's beauty? I look at it as a gift, a way of showing my love for my friends and family and perhaps enriching their day by causing a brief pause in their busy lives to awe at a flash of nature's wonder.

Parties with a seasonal theme give a great excuse for more elaborate decoration. And you don't have to restrict yourself to the obvious celebrations, such as Christmas and Hallowe'en. Different cultures have their own traditions. The Japanese have cherry blossom parties in the spring, when friends and family gather under the trees to watch the blossoms fall. Celebrate on a smaller scale by bringing in a few stems of cherry blossom indoors and placing them in a jug on your kitchen table to force them into bloom. At the height of summer celebrate the solstice as the Swedish do. Make daisy chains, have everyone wear white, freeze vodka and serve it with fresh edible flowers such as bright orange and red nasturtiums with their peppery petals. In the autumn hold a harvest festival dinner. To create a completely different informal dining atmosphere use a pallet or a low coffee table covered with a big cloth or kilim and surround it with all the cushions in the house for seating. Go over the top with candles by placing them on every appropriate surface and let them serve as your only lighting. Serve pumpkin soup out of a hollowed-out pumpkin.

Changing your dining table can be achieved simply with the throw of a cloth and a centrepiece that reflects the season. Usually natural elements work the best. A dining table can be transformed for an event with the simple throw of a tablecloth. Different patterns and textures lend themselves to different times of year.

A small outside space becomes an informal eating area in summer. **top far left** The chandelier will be brought inside to warm the house in winter but here it gets an airing and provides a frame for pots of flowers. **bottom far left** A tumbler is filled to bursting with small sprigs and flower heads plucked from the garden. **left** Layers of textiles set a scene conducive to a long afternoon's relaxation. **above** The vibrant colours of the kilims and robust canvas cushion covers reflect the palette of the garden.

107

right and opposite Textiles added or subtracted as the weather dictates make a distinctive change in the mood of this room. Even the smallest change such as the objects on this mantel incite a moment's contemplation and add to the stimulating feel of a house that is very much in motion. **above** An artful juxtoposition of textures and shapes makes for intriguing still lifes. **far right** A summer story of whites is made up of such incongruous items as a candle, a jug of flowers from the garden and a necklace.

For instance, gingham always looks fresh in the spring-time alongside a jug of daffodils. Layering cloths can take a textile from one season into another. A pretty white embroidered tablecloth looks light and airy in summer but can be layered over something more textural such as a rough linen sheet when cooler weather calls for something more substantial. Dining chairs can be a group of mismatched second-hand market finds, perhaps painted all one colour for unity. Even the humblest dining chair can look elegant when it is dressed up in a home-made slipcover.

Dreaming and refreshing

THE BEDROOM IS OUR MOST PERSONAL SPACE. IT CONTAINS OUR MOST INTIMATE THOUGHTS AND POSSESSIONS AND STAYS VEILED FROM THE VIEW OF THE OUTSIDE WORLD. IT IS A HAVEN WITHIN THE HAVEN OF HOME, THE SAFEST PLACE WITHIN A SAFE PLACE. A BEDROOM IS WHERE OUR DREAMS AND IMAGINATIONS CAN FEEL SECURE ENOUGH TO FLOAT AS FAR AS THEY CAN GO. Creativity is without boundaries and our thoughts can have full sway. It should be a room that harbours intimacy, allowing you to truly be yourself. It is a place to retreat to rejuvenate; to be alone with your thoughts. More than any other activity the patterns of sleep are linked into nature's cycle. The changing lengths of day and nights affect our circadian rhythms, so that in the depths of winter we struggle from sleep when the alarm wakes us, but in summer, sunlight awakens us more gently. The intimacy of a bedroom allows for a certain vulnerability. It is said that chidren's minds are most open just before they fall asleep. Have you ever stayed awake in the darkness with a child, friend or lover just talking? Somehow the security of a bedroom and the blanket of darkness allows for this type of openness, where the barriers we put up around us to face the outside world can be taken down, allowing our minds to just drift.

Layers of cashmere throws and pillows in a variety of colours become a vehicle to adapt the mood of a bed from one season to the next. **above** Sherbet colours suggest summer fruits and berries. **right** Mosquito netting transforms an otherwise functional sleeping area into a romantic summer retreat. **opposite** A layer of basic white bed linen is versatile enough to carry different looks throughout the year. **top far right** Soft cashmere pajamas offer the ultimate in winter comfort and luxury. **bottom far right** Small bedside posies pick up the changing colours.

The bedroom is where your whole mind and body come into repose. To make an atmosphere that is conducive to this feelings surround yourself only with things that make you feel good. This is the place where you can really indulge your senses with tactile fabrics, soothing scents, harmonious colours and soulful music. The proper lighting is essential to the mood, and a dimmer switch is a great idea in the bedroom as it can easily change the space from a practical one where you apply your make-up to a romantic or restful one. Satisfy your physical need to be comforted. In winter when the weather is dull, a huge knitted bed throw of the softest yarn and an amaryllis blooming

on the radiator may be all that is needed to chase the winter blues away. In summer a cool breezy atmosphere with simple white bed linen and the scent of lavender drifting in from an open window can be a welcome relief after a long hot day.

Working as a fashion designer, I use fabric and accessories in a seasonal way. I love the anticipation of each coming season, changing my wardrobe from winter woollens to spring cottons and summer linens. Therefore it was only natural for me to approach my home in a seasonal manner also. I realized my rooms should change like my wardrobe did. And just as in my wardrobe I have my basics, I have them for my home also. Year round, fine white bedding works as a base for a soothing restful look. Onto this layer textures and patterns as your mood dictates. Gone are the days when we thought we had to have a matching set of sheets. Pile layers on as the weather gets colder and peel them off as the warm weather arrives. Think of it as putting together a wardrobe for your bed.

The simplest way to change the feel of a bedroom is by changing the bed linen. A fresh duvet cover especially can, in one bold stroke, change the entire look of the room. Unfortunately, really attractive ones are hard to track down and they can be unbelievably expensive.

When decorating with an all white palette, texture plays an important role in reflecting the changing seasons. **far left** Space is one of the biggest luxuries we have today. The all-white palette and sparse furnishings of this room exaggerate the space, lending the room a calm and peaceful feeling. **centre left** Functional metal mugs and a florist's bucket used as vases lend a certain no-nonsense approach to decorating. In contrast to this the flower sprigs add softness and a heavenly

aroma to fill the room. **centre right** The clean mimimal atmosphere of the room remains constant through the year but in readiness for cooler weather there are piles of throws and bed covers. Enormous cushions will be propped up at the end of the bed for comfortable night-time reading. **above** A play of textures – juxtaposing the luxury of a cashmere throw and mohair blanket against the sparseness of the room – makes for a sensuous mix of hard against soft.

top far left The smallest touch can hint at a season. A bedside posy of a few narcissus buds is replaced by a favourite postcard, evoking an earthy feel in the winter months (far left).
bottom far left A dress caught momentarily hanging from the door becomes a temporary still life, a play of light and shadow. **left** Thin pure cotton bed covers are light and easy in summer. **below** A fur throw maintains the look without sacrificing comfort.

Try making your own covers by sewing two sheets together, perhaps adding a linen flange around the edge such as you would find on a pillow case. Or try making one in a patchwork of leftover fabrics. Likewise, inexpensive simple white cotton sheets and pillow cases can be personalized with trimmings such as adding piqué boarders at the edges, or a pretty ribbon running along the top – even some antique buttons added as a closure on a pillow case can give a special twist. Work with contrasts: if you decide you want a romantic bed with piles of white lace ruffles complement this by keeping the rest of the room bare for drama.

Look to your wardrobe, not only to find the key to your style, but as a source of

Create wardrobes for your bed that evolve from season to season

accessories for your home. A collection of bead necklaces need not be relegated to a jewellery box but can be put on display hanging from a door knob, or even used as curtain tie-backs. Similarly, a beautiful scarf or shawl can be displayed simply hanging from a nail in the wall. Group your jewellery and accessories neatly in a row of shallow baskets and place them on a bench against one wall for easy access. You can get as much pleasure from displaying favourite items from your wardrobe and looking at them every day as you do from wearing them. Resist the temptation to go out and buy new things for your home when there is a whole box of goodies tucked away in your closet.

Walking into this bedroom feels like
going on a summer holiday. **below,
from left** A mixture of junk shop
furniture has all been painted white for
a more cohesive look. The palest aqua
hints at summer skies. Casual touches
such as shirts hanging from pegs on
the wall reflect the laid-back lifestyle of
summer. **right** Small incidental flowers
are as effective as large displays and
lend themselves to the effortless air of
this summer room.

One of my most cherished moments of the day is the earliest hours of the morning when my husband and I are woken by the sound of small feet making their way into our bedroom. Our two little boys sleepily climb into bed with us and we all start the day slowly waking up together. Sometimes we just sit in silence together, sometimes there are giggles and tea cups have been known to topple onto the bed. For me it is the most cherished moment of day. I love the thought that, without fail, every morning the bed my husband and I share becomes a family bed. Those few moments work as a point of contact

The Scandinavian feel of this room works just as well in hot and cold weather. The cool blue colours evoke a winter's landscape and easily become a seaside memory in summer. **opposite** Paper snowflake cut-outs echo the gently falling snow outside. **above, from left** the first glimpse of a simple pose of a few objects from the doorway of a room sets the tone for what is around the corner. Vintage blankets with wonderfully mellowed colours from

years of frequent washing. The bed is piled with warm woolly blankets and plenty of pillows to snuggle into on a winter night. **below, from left** The cushion covers are handmade with easy linen ties for closure. In the summer months seaside stripes in cotton come out of storage to replace the winter woollens, turning this bedroom into a cool retreat. Woven rope shoes easily make the move from the beach indoors.

for us as a family before we all venture out into the larger world. It is at moments like these in the intimacy of our bed that I truly feel the value of the sense of security and shelter that our home brings to us.

Small gestures that are meaningful to you are what make your house a home. Your bedside table tells the story of what is currently going on in your life. Fill it with a selection of books to lose yourself in, a scented candle and a favourite postcard or photo. Small indulgent touches such as flowers by your bedside can make you feel especially pampered – I suppose it is the thought that they are there for only you to enjoy that makes them feel so luxurious.

Years ago my husband gave me a watercolour sketchbook in which he had painted a series of land- and sky scapes. I keep it on the mantelpiece next to my mirror in my bedroom and change the page according to the season and my mood. In summer my favourite page is a light and airy painting of clouds, in winter I tend to turn the page to one of the more earthy landscapes he painted of the ploughed red fields of England. Not only is it a treasured gift, something that I love to look at every morning, but it also works as a reminder of the changing landscapes outside. It works as a personal touchstone for me as this is a place I come to at least once in my daily routine.

Bathrooms should be viewed just as indulgently as bedrooms, for they are equally personal spaces. We rarely think to place flowers here, but just a few sprays of eucalyptus or one or two sweet peas in a tooth mug next to the basin will give a lift to your spirits first thing in the morning and last thing at night when you brush your teeth, and the steamy atmosphere will bring out their scent. Bathrooms naturally lend themselves to a summery treatment, perhaps because the associations with water suggest a blue or green colour treatment. But they can be transformed into winter havens with an abundance of thick fleecy towels and generous amounts of candlelight.

Borrowing from fashion adds a playful sense of surprise in this bedroom throughout the year. **above, from left** Vintage handkerchiefs are stitched onto brightly coloured throw cushions. The white pillow cases are made from plain white sheeting, with grandma's old lace cocktail napkins appliquéd on the front. A jam jar is used temporarily as a vase, filled with geraniums that make economical and lasting cut flowers. A love note pressed between glass with rose petals stays by the bedside table.

A wreath fashioned from branches collected in an apple orchard is a token of winter and the completion of the year. A slightly irreverent mix of pattern keeps the room from becoming too serious. A warm blanket was made by stitching together large squares of cream wool. The bedside table gets cluttered with winter's activities and interests: sketches are taped casually on the wall to allow for an easy change of scenery. Drawstring bags are made from vintage clothing.

this page Sometimes a room stays in one season all year; the double aspect of this small bathroom ensures that it is flooded with light all year round. Light linen cafe curtains allow for privacy without hindering the light streaming in or the view. The shower curtain is fashioned from a sheer embroidered cotton lined with plastic and adorned with old curtain clips found in a second-hand market. **opposite** A space is transformed with candlelight, making a winter's bath a soul-sustaining ritual. A bit of pampering is a much-needed escape when the weather turns harsh.

Source directory

Furniture and Accessories

After Noah
261 Kings Road
London SW3 5EL
0171 359 4281
An eclectic mix of antique and contemporary furniture and household items

The Blue Door
77 Church Road
London SW13 9HH
0181 748 9785
Handpainted furniture from the Gustavian period; textiles and accessories with a simple Swedish spirit

The Conran Shop
Michelin House
81 Fulham Road
London SW3 6RD
0171 589 7401
Everything for the home

Castle Gibson
106a Upper Street
London N1 1QN
0171 704 0927
Antiques shop specializing in school house, industrial and office furniture

The Cross
141 Portland Road
London W11 4LR
0171 727 6760
Small but inspiring shop with a bath department and a few well-chosen accessories for the home

Designers Guild
261–71 King's Road
London SW3 5EN
0171 243 7300
Cheerful mix of fabric, furniture and decorative items

Egg
36 Kinnerton Street
London SW1X 8ER
0171 235 9315
Eclectic personal mix of home accessories with a strong ethnic influence

Habitat
196 Tottenham Court Road
London W1P 9LD
0171 631 3880
Great one-stop shop for the home and garden; especially strong for bed linen, picture frames and lighting

John Lewis
278–306 Oxford Street
London W1 1EX
0171 629 7711
Best department store for haberdashery and curtain accessories

Jerry's Home Store
163–67 Fulham Road
London SW3 6SN
0171 581 0909
Great basics with an American flair; especially strong kitchen department

Cath Kidston
8 Clarendon Cross
London W11 4AP
0171 221 4000
Range of household products, fabrics and wallpapers inspired by 1950s prints as well as a selection of vintage textiles

Liberty
214–20 Regent Street
London W1 6AH
0171 734 1234
Excellent haberdashery and fabric; also great for bath and kitchen accessories

Michael Lewis Antiques
16 Essex Road
London N1 8LN
0171 727 3908
Wonderful selection of country furniture

Catherine Memmi
33–34 Rue St Suplice
Paris 75006
France
001 44 072226
Clean well-designed homewares; especially strong on table and bed linens

Muji
187 Oxford Street
London W1R 1AJ
Japanese simple and functional household goods, including a good range of storage items

Parma Lilac
0181 960 9239
Children's nursery furnishings and accessories

Ruffle & Hook
122–24 St Johns Street
London EC1V 4JS
0171 490 4321
Soft modern collection of home accessories and textiles

Sanderson
112–20 Brompton Road
London SW3 1JJ
0171 584 3344
Fabric, wallpaper and paints

Stanley Supply Store
48 Emu Rd
London SW8 3PH
0171 627 2999
Simple chic range of household accessories

STORY
0171 288 0388
Fantastic new conceptual shop with a well-chosen personal mix of things for the home – earthy, rustic and sensual

Summerill & Bishop
100 Portland Road
London W11 4LN
071 221 4566
Great selection of kitchen and cooking accessories

Tobias & the Angel
66–68 White Hart Lane
London SW13 0PZ
0181 878 8902
Simple country furniture, quilts and well-chosen bric-à-brac

David Wainwright
61–63 Portobello Road
London W11 3DB
0171 727 0707
Indian furniture and accessories

Textiles

The Berwick Street Cloth Shop
14 Berwick Street
London W1V 3RG
0171 287 2881
Fashion fabrics but great for the home; good selection of velvets

Borovick Fabrics Ltd
16 Berwick Street
London W1V 4HP
0171 437 2180
Suppliers of fabrics for stage
screen and TV; unusual finds

Ian Mankin
271 Wandsworth Bridge Road
London SW6 2TX
0171 371 8825
Great value for stylish simple
textiles, cottons, sheers,
stripes and checks

Natural Fabric Company
Wessex Place
127 High Street
Hungerford
Berkshire RG17 0DL
01488 684002
Natural fabrics at reasonable
prices, plus haberdashery; mail
order catologue

Jane Sacchi
7 Markham Street
London SW3 3NP
0171 589 5643
(by appointment only)
Selection of antique French
textiles including tickings,
fine linen sheets and
wonderful tea towels

Textile King
81 Berwick Street
London W1V 3PF
0171 437 7372
Gent's suiting specialist; good
source of woollens, tweeds and
shirting fabrics

Bryony Thomasson
283 Westbourne Grove
Portobello Road Market
London W11 (Sat mornings)
or 0171 731 3693
(by appointment only)
Antique textiles, grain sacks,
and hand-woven linen sheets

Wolfin Textiles
64 Great Titchfield Street
London W1P 7AE
0171 636 4949
Great value for money on basic
fabrics including calicos,
sheeting and ticking

Specialist Paint

Farrow & Ball
33 Uddens Estate
Wimborne
Dorset BH21 7NL
01202 876141
Wonderful muted colours; the
National Trust range of paints

John Oliver
33 Pembridge Road
London W11 3HG
0171 727 3735
A wide range of specialist
paints, with a beautiful chalky
quality in the emulsion

Paint Library
25 Draycott Place
London SW3 2SH
0171 823 7755
Soft modern colour range and
unusual finishes

Specialist Shops

The Bead Shop
43 Neal Street
London WC2 9PJ
0171 240 0931
Inspiring collection of beads

Arthur Beale Ltd
194 Shaftesbury Avenue
London WC2H 8JP
0171 836 9034
Yacht chandlers; inspiring shop
for hardware and rope, full of
ideas that can be used for the
home

Celestial Buttons
54 Cross Street
London N1 2BA
0171 226 4766
Broad range of buttons for
personalizing soft furnishings

LASSCo
Architectural Salvage
St Micheal's
Mark Street
London EC2 4ER
0171 739 0448
Large selection of salvaged
items, from fire places to door
knobs

Pentonville Rubber Company
104 Pentonville Road
London N1 9JB
0171 837 4582
Cushions and foam cut to any
size you want

V.V. Rouleaux
10 Symons Street
London SW3 2TJ
0171 730 4413
Inspiring collection of ribbons

Art Supply Shops

Atlantis Art
146 Brick Lane
London E16 6RU
0171 377 8855
Fantastic selection of fine art
supplies, including all weights
of linen and canvas and a large
range of handmade papers

Paperchase
213 Tottenham Court Road
London W1P 9AF
0171 580 8496
The best source for all types of
paper and stationery

Russell & Chapple Ltd
23 Monmouth Street
London WC2H 9DE
0171 836 7521
All weights of canvas, cottons
and linens

Markets

Bermondsey Market
Bermondsey Square
London SE1
Friday mornings: junk furniture,
household accessories

Camden Passage Antiques
Market
Upper Street
London N1
Wednesday and Saturday
mornings: good for buttons,
cutlery and various bric-à-brac

Columbia Road Flower Market
Columbia Road
London E1
Sunday mornings: great fun and
value for bulbs, bedding plants,
herbs and cut flowers

Portobello Road Market
Portobello Road/
Westbourne Grove
London W11
Friday and Saturday mornings:
large market with everything
from furniture to antique
prints and 20th-century
clothing

Acknowledgements

Thanks to the following people for their help
with this book:

Victoria Bailey for her creative spirit
Angela Miller for her endless support
Lisa Hoss Panitz for her enthusiam
Sian Parkhouse for her dedication
Jacqui Small for her vision
James Merrell for his eye

Thanks to everyone at Ryland Peters & Small.

A big thanks to everyone who so graciously opened their
homes to be photographed for this book and who each in
turn was an inspiration: Ann Shore, K. Russell Glover and
Angela Miller, Tom Fallon, Sig Bergamin, Gabriele Sanders,
Katsuji Asada, Janet and Hiroshi Kazo, Janie Jackson, Barbara
Davis and her family, Liz Dougherty Pierce.

But especially to Dave, Josh and Ben for . . . well, just about
everything.

The publishers would like to acknowledge the work of Janie Jackson,
stylist/designer, whose work appears on the front cover and on page 94 top
right, pages 86–87, and pages 114–17, and the work of William and Barbara
Davis, designer, New York State (telephone 607-264-3673), whose work
appears on page 4 centre, page 34 left and bottom left, page 41 upper right
and lower right, page 78, page 100 and pages 120–21.